The Family History Fun Factor

How to Gather and Preserve Family Folklore

Marcha Fox

KALLIOPE RISING PRESS

NAPLES, NEW YORK

PRINT ISBN: 978-0-988-3335-9-8

EBOOK ISBN: 978-0-9883335-3-6

Printed in USA

First Printing: October 2015

Cover and interior design by the author

Photographs from the author's personal archives

Published by:

Kalliope Rising Press

Naples, New York

14512

Contents

Other Titles

Star Trails Science Fiction Adventure Series

Beyond the Hidden Sky*

A Dark of Endless Days*

A Psilent Place Below*

Refractions of Frozen Time*

The Star Trails Tetralogy Box Set

The Sapphiran Agenda*

The Terra Debacle: Prisoners at Area 51*

The Star Trails Compendium

Available as audiobooks narrated by T. W. Ashworth

StarTrailsSaga.com

The Curse of Dead Horse Canyon Trilogy

With co-author, Pete Risingsun

The Curse of Dead Horse Canyon: Cheyenne Spirits

Return to Dead Horse Canyon: Grandfather Spirits

Revenge of Dead Horse Canyon: Sweet Medicine Spirits - Novavose

The Curse of Dead Horse Canyon Trilogy: A Cheyenne Saga of Retribution

Dead-Horse-Canyon.com

Introduction

WHAT WOULD YOU GIVE to spend a day with one of your ancestors? To witness everyday details of his or her life, whether it involved a favorite recipe, cooking methods, shopping, transportation, or how children spent their day?

Genealogy and stories related to major life events such as immigration, migrations, arranged marriages, childbirth, deaths or occupations can often be found in journals or other sources. But what about everyday activities such as holiday celebrations or the games children played on balmy summer evenings? Wouldn't you like to go one step beyond walking four miles to school through two feet of snow or canning peaches on a woodstove?

Unfortunately, modern science hasn't given us anything but theories regarding a time machine or other means to accomplish such a feat. Given that, following time's arrow in the other direction back to your progenitors isn't going to happen anytime soon. Don't you think your descendants might wonder the same things about you? Even if you're diligently keeping records current regarding births, deaths and marriages, what will they learn about your everyday life? Have you included what it was like before cell phones, texting, the internet, satellite radio, and iPads? Along similar lines, what would you include if you were to create a time capsule to be opened a hundred years from now?

Such things comprise an oft-neglected element that makes family members more memorable, colorful, and human. It has a name you've undoubtedly heard but probably in a broader context that didn't seem to relate to your family or situation. Any idea what it is? Here's another hint: Collecting it is fun and even more entertaining as the years go by. Furthermore, it's something kids can participate in *now* which will not only make them feel important and cultivate interest but be enjoyed as much as those vacation pictures twenty years from now.

Figure it out yet? Yes, recipes are included but it goes beyond that. It actually has an official name and is specifically taught in universities such as Utah State and North Dakota State who also maintain collections of this historically significant information.

Give up?

Okay, I'll get to the point. The answer: *Family Folklore.*

The definition offered by 4-H organizations is "Family Folklore is the way your family captures its experiences and keeps its past alive." If that isn't specific enough to suit you, the Western States Arts Federation (WESTAF) provides a bit more detail:

Folklife traditions are expressions of a shared culture, acquired and passed on over time in face-to-face interaction and in small groups (through oral tradition, performance, etc.). Groups share folklife on the basis of their ethnicity, religion, occupation, gender, region, family membership, or any other kind of common identity. While folklife is maintained over generations, it changes as tradition bearers adapt to changing cultural circumstances and exercise creativity within the conventions of a form of folklife. Forms of folklife include customs, beliefs, traditional narrative, folk songs, vernacular architecture, traditional crafts, festivals, folk theatre, rituals, traditional folk dances, etc. All can be found in cultures worldwide.[1]

I'll bet you thought folklore was limited to the world of myth and superstition. Things like fairies, ghosts, leprechauns, and tales of Robin Hood or King Arthur.

But guess what?

It's not.

Your family has a wealth of it, including the stories you've already collected. And that's what this book is all about, finding those family jewels hiding in plain sight by taking you through several categories/genres to trigger your memory and imagination so you can capture another dimension of life that deserves preservation every bit as much as those boring vital statistics.

---

1. http://www.westaf.org/resources/folklife accessed 8/30/2013 (Western States Arts Federation)

CHAPTER ONE

Collection Methods

*H*OW YOU PRESERVE THESE treasures is entirely up to you. It's best to do it the easiest way and have *something* as opposed to procrastinating because it's too much trouble, then losing it forever. If you're already into family history, then I don't need to tell you *how*.

However, if you're so busy working and raising a family that your family history comprises a shoebox in the closet of that spare bedroom (if you're lucky enough to have one) or perhaps a folder on your computer desktop where all those unorganized photos reside, that's better than nothing. At least you have something to start with when life calms down. Just don't make it complicated. That's the fastest way to condemn it to total failure.

The vast majority of folklore categories can be collected in a variety of ways made relatively simple by the advent of media such as voice recorders, videos and digital recordkeeping. Of course, photography works for most types along with written descriptions. The scrapbooking craze has also provided a creative means to make your family's history more appealing than pedigree charts and dry narratives as captivating as *so-and-so begat so-and-so* litanies in the Bible.

Your creativity is an important part of the entire process, not only because it makes it more fun and interesting, but because your personality will be implicit in it as well. Chances are you've already implemented some or all of those modern innovations to liven things up. After all, as much fun as it may be as a hobby, why put in all that work if no one else is going to enjoy it?

Using today's technology simplifies the process significantly. For example, the next time you see grandpa use your smart phone to record one of his favorite stories. Better yet, make it a video. Having family stories preserved as told by their originator with his or her voice and inflections is undoubtedly more valuable and easier to obtain than a sketchy or poorly written summary. How many volumes of history have been lost for lack of writing skill or the discipline to keep a journal or record important events? However, some people can't tell a joke much less a story and there's no guarantee grandpa can tell it better than you could capture it in writing.

The main point is to preserve it *somehow.* Even if his rendition isn't worthy of a university oral history archive, you can always use the recording later to write it up, if you're so inclined. On the other hand, no matter how poor his storytelling skills may be, it still represents an authentic grandpa, which conveys him and his personality to say nothing of his voice which otherwise will be lost to all but memory of those who knew him personally. Even if he was a horrible storyteller I would LOVE to hear my grandfathers' voices, both of whom died before I was born. Wouldn't you?

If the person of interest isn't a great orator as far as stories are concerned, another approach is to get them talking about the "good ol' days." The section on categories can arm you with plenty of conversation starters a little more specific than "What did you do before TV?"

The polish of your finished product depends on your talents and/or training with formatting and editing as well as your level of ambition. If any of these are limited, at this point you might want to employ a family member more savvy than yourself with the media involved. This helps recruit additional participants and generate enthusiasm, often crossing generations in the process. If you have any project management skills, you may be able to get today's tech-savvy youth involved which will make your job even easier as they'll do the collecting and packaging, then send it to you in an email.

CHAPTER TWO

Social Media

*J*F YOU'RE A FACEBOOK, Pinterest, or X (previously Twitter) fan, the good news is that you're already in the folklore game, even if you didn't realize it. Think for just a moment about how much online social media is part of your everyday life. Has it become natural or what? How many birthday parties, vacations, recipes or special events are out there? Now take it a step further. How much more time would it take to include that same information in a folder on your desktop? A minute or two perhaps? Another click or two and you're on your way. See how easy it could be? And it's that everyday stuff that's most likely to contain the true essence of life.

At this point I want to make a point or two for any Baby Boomers who are finally retired and have time and inclination to compile their family history. While you undoubtedly have a computer or perhaps even a Kindle if you're reading this, you may be preserving your memories the old-fashioned way by relying on old photos accompanied by some written narrative to capture your life. That is definitely a good thing, which I'll go into more detail about below, but paper is expected to disappear at some point in the near future, possibly sooner than you care to consider.

The good news is that scrapbooks and old-fashioned picture albums will be even more precious due to their antique value even if they're bulkier to store.

Nonetheless, identifying your audience is the first rule of writing or any other form of communication, for that matter. With that in mind, your children, grandchildren and great-grandchildren will be more receptive to all your hard work if they can access it (and deliver it) in a familiar format.

Thus, it will benefit you as well as them if you familiarize yourself with the media explosion in which the younger generation is immersed; Facebook and YouTube are a way of life.

Some Baby Boomers are extremely tech-literate with their iPhones and such, but others are downright phobic and refuse to even own a computer, much less anything else, no doubt intimidated by the complexity of today's electronic world. If you want to get involved, consider asking a member of the younger generation for help. That will not only help you figure it out, but involve them as well.

At this point, however, let me offer a nickel's worth of free advice on how to ask. If you say something too vague, such as "Show me how to use this computer" you're likely to get a classic deer-in-the-headlights stare. However, if you say "Show me your favorite YouTube video" you should get a slightly better response. I don't know about your children and grandchildren, but I think mine were born with computer literacy in their DNA. If they grew up with video games, computers and so forth their operation is intuitive and they probably can't explain it.

Visual and kinesthetic learning prevails in their world, so explaining such things verbally usually goes beyond their cognizant and language skills. However, if you let them show you, then maybe convince them to let you try it under their direction, you're more likely to be successful. For example, if you decide to take the plunge and get on Facebook, have one of them help you set it up as well as the basics of posting comments and pictures.

While it's important to preserve your history to represent a different generation and time, you should also encourage your children and grandchildren to record their memories now. More than likely they're into social media, which could mean their family history is getting lost in the ever-scrolling timeline world of Facebook. Life happens one day at a time and even as what's news today will be tomorrow's history, so is the stuff of life. With the ease of taking photos and creating voice or video recordings introduced by smart phones, the younger generation is already on their way to compiling their personal history. Not only could they teach you something about it, they'll be a lot more impressed with yours if you close that gap.

CHAPTER THREE

Beware of Obsolescence

*N*OW I'M GOING TO contradict much of what I've said previously, but I believe it's something you need to know. As great as all those devices are don't forget how quickly they can become obsolete. Imagine finding a stack of 5 ¼ inch floppy disks and cassette tapes much less eight-millimeter home movies in grandma's cedar chest and what you'd have to go through to extract whatever they contained.

When you use technology, you have to continually transfer the data to the next generation device or it could be lost forever, as you may have already discovered if you use genealogical software. Conversely, if the Mayan's and various prophecies are right, civilization as we know it could disappear off the face of the Earth, instituting the opposite problem. Various programs on the History Channel talk about those mysterious crystal skulls like the ones in the last Indiana Jones movie and propose they may contain some sort of ancient record, presenting the same problem of data extraction from the opposite end of the technological timeline.

Boring as it may be, paper remains the most reliable record source provided you use acid free and store it properly, preferably in a low humidity environment. Like Egyptian papyri and the Dead Sea Scrolls, if it's on paper it can always be read. Therefore, whatever you write or scan should be printed out at some point, unless you want to keep upgrading the media or maintain a computer museum *ad infinitum*. Some progress has been made toward file format standardization but even that could change at any time with the next technological breakthrough.

We may yet figure out those crystal skulls!

This technological generation gap could mean that all your hard work is either ignored or imprisoned on a CD or memory stick that can't be read by some future device. Permanence today is more than using acid-free paper and offers an enchanting array of options that make your efforts all the more detailed and interesting, now and to future generations. If you don't feel like taking on Facebook or YouTube that's understandable, but be sure to talk to someone who's tech savvy regarding how to preserve your digital work so it won't be overcome by obsolescence and be for naught.

Software is continually updated as well, making it even more difficult to assure all your hard work will be accessible twenty or more years from now. Certain file formats such as pdf and rtf provide some continuity through standardization, but as you probably already know, life has no guarantees. Thus, continually updating old records is essential as well as keeping a few hardcopies (printouts) unless you want to resort to that defunct computer museum as part of your story. Do you still have a box of old movies on video cassette? Can you still watch them? *Capisce?*

That said, let's move onto the good stuff. The following categories should trigger your imagination for what is out there awaiting capture but the most important rule is to make it fun and include as much everyday life as possible.

CHAPTER FOUR

Categories/Genres

YOU MAY NOT BE surprised to know that there are dozens of categories. Thus, if existing ones don't fit what you have, then invent more! Folklore is everywhere, once you realize it's there. Have you ever watched the show *American Pickers* on The History Channel? Talk about folklore! They're living it!

Consider for a moment how interesting it would be to go back to the 18th or 19th century and visit your great-great-great grandparents in their home. If you're lucky enough to have a few old pictures, you've no doubt imagined what their house and daily life was like. Probably one of the biggest changes between then and now is the lack of electricity.

Consider writing letters that took weeks or months to arrive, versus the instantaneous worldwide delivery of email, texting or tweeting. How about witnessing news on distant continents via satellite as it happens versus waiting for such information to arrive via the nearest big city's newspaper? Or driving to Wal*mart to pick up a few things, versus a monthly horse and buggy ride to the town country store? All illustrate how quickly things can change.

Someday soon everything might be delivered to your door by a drone.

Past generations, such as my mother who was born in 1906, grew up with a horse and buggy, yet lived to see men walk on the Moon and the wonder of the Internet. Think for a moment what you've witnessed in your lifetime. I remember giving a talk one time to a group of Boy Scouts about the space shuttle and my job at NASA. One of them asked if any of them had ever crashed. At first I thought, *How could he have possibly missed* that *on the news?*

Then I realized it occurred before he was even born! What historical events have you witnessed about which your feelings and impressions should be preserved for your posterity? Writing up my experiences in the aerospace industry as a contractor at NASA's Johnson Space Center in Houston is definitely on my to-do list, such as the sad task of picking up debris from *Columbia* in East Texas.

Do you think that technological progress is going to stop? Of course not, unless perhaps the Mayans were right along with various others who profess doom and gloom scenarios. The point I'm trying to make is that your everyday life *now* may be as strange to someone fifty years down the road as the 1960s would be to kids today.

In your family history memorabilia do you have at least one daybook that provides a glimpse of what life was like in the 1800s? Your daily routine may seem less than exciting and not worth recording, but to someone in the far distant future it could hold as much charm and interest as life a few centuries ago does for you.

The best way to preserve it goes beyond the calendar where you keep track of your appointments or record when it rains. And that's what the following categories are all about, reminding you of the fascinating activities all around you that will be of interest of others in another lifetime.

Family Stories

These encompass everything from soup to nuts. You probably already include your favorite stories in your family history. If not, it's time you did. Funny stories, particularly those that illustrate the personality of an individual, are especially important and valuable. Examples from the past include such things as when Uncle Al fell head-first into the outhouse or Great-grandpa pulled the plow with his Model T. And speaking of cars, often there's a great story behind the automobiles in your life, too!

Not all family stories are amusing, but as a rule the serious ones are usually included more readily than the other side of life. For example, war stories are usually at the top of the list. What makes you laugh, however, is every bit as important as what makes you cry. What better way to really know someone than through their sense of humor?

Everyone has stories associated with holiday gatherings, whether it's when all the brothers/uncles wound up on the front lawn in a brawl after Thanksgiving dinner or Grandma's last Christmas when everyone gathered at the resthome. Thus, this is a good place to look for fable fodder.

"Where were you when" stories for major events are always of interest, whether the event was tragic or celebratory. These include such things as the John F. Kennedy assassination, Space Shuttle *Challenger* or *Columbia* disasters, September 11, 2001, or societal changes incident to the COVID-19 pandemic. While those examples are on the dark side, attending a championship game, Indianapolis 500, Superbowl, or some other exciting event are on the light side. But the special ones aren't the only possibility. Simple traditions count as well.

The *Family Folklore Idea Collection Sheet* in Appendix A includes numerous memory joggers as well as hints to help you assemble needed details. See how many you can fill in. It can come in handy for interviews, too.

You can get an electronic copy of this table for free by sending an email with "FHFF Idea Collection Sheet" in the subject line to *marcha@kallioperisingpress.com*. I'll send you one in pdf format that will make it even easier to send a copy to family members to gather their memories, too.

Meanwhile, this should get your creative juices flowing, though by now you shouldn't have any doubts what a wealth of information specific to your family is just waiting for someone to capture it.

Foodways

This category includes recipes but goes beyond that. Does everyone in your family like their steak medium rare except for one who likes it well-done? You've probably heard the story about cutting off the ends of the roast prior to cooking.

In case you haven't, it involved a daughter asking her mother why she always cut off the ends of the roast before putting it in the pan. She said because *her* mother always did it. When she followed up by asking her grandmother, she found out it was because it was the only way it would fit in the pan.

Did Auntie Jewel make the worst gravy in the history of the world? What family food traditions were there? Smoked brisket on the Fourth of July? Green bean casserole on Thanksgiving? Black-eyed peas on New Years Day?

When I first got married, I was a stark traditionalist. Thus, when I got roped into having Christmas dinner for the family because we were the only ones with a house I went way overboard making everything from scratch. I planned to stick to traditional recipes, such as pumpkin and mince pies, which had been traditions in my own family that hailed from the East Coast.

This did not fly with my husband or his family, who were dyed-in-the-wool Californians. I was entirely scandalized to have chocolate cream pie for Christmas, but I acquiesced. And after twenty years of making chocolate cream pie for Christmas dinner, guess what? We'd created our own tradition!

One holiday-specific meal that my family enjoyed was for Halloween. I had a less than fancy casserole I used to make on a regular basis that comprised hamburger, potatoes, carrots and cream of mushroom soup. Yum, right? Anyway, I got the bright idea to hollow out a small pumpkin from the garden, carve a face on it, fill it with the casserole, and bake it in the oven. (The pumpkin takes quite a while to cook, by the way, if you're thinking of trying this.) When it's finished, the casserole is drooling out of the eyes and mouth in a disgusting enough way to please the kids and the pumpkin tastes like squash, which is delicious with butter, salt, and pepper, creating a healthy yet fun meal to prepare the kids for trick-or-treating.

Christmas and Thanksgiving are usually no-brainers, but I'll bet most people never document the recipes that form their most savory traditions. If they're anything like mine, they're scattered all over in various cookbooks, bundles of random magazine clippings, and an ancient recipe box that belonged to my mother.

Does your family enjoy picnics? What simply *had* to be included, or it wasn't a proper picnic? What about the Fourth of July? Did you feast on the usual hot dogs and hamburgers on the grill or a smoked brisket or turkey? What about Aunt Hannah's famous potato salad or the time the watermelon fermented, unless it was spiked by Uncle Jake?

When we first moved to Texas, we spent our first Fourth of July in the nextdoor neighbor's pool watching the fireworks display at the high school stadium a block away. After that we'd walk over with an ice chest filled with our favorite ice cream to eat during the festivities. Then they built a subdivision in the undeveloped area where the fireworks were previously ignited from, extinguishing that tradition for all concerned.

Food not only sustains life but also feeds your traditions. Traditional recipes handed down from generation to generation should most definitely be included. Poll the family and compile a listing of their favorite dishes, another activity everyone can enjoy.

Trip, Location, and Transportation

Was there one particular place that you celebrated a certain holiday or anniversary each year? Was it close by or a major excursion? Did you fly, take a cruise, drive, or walk? Did everything go as planned? Travel problems often make great stories later, like that seventeen-hour layover sleeping on the floor in the Atlanta airport due to a hurricane, the time the transmission went out fifteen miles out of Flagstaff, when the fan belt broke in the middle of the Nevada desert, or simply the convenience of walking a block or two to enjoy Fourth of July fireworks. Was getting there half the fun or the worst part?

Which vehicle survived one or more family members learning to drive? How many times did they have to take the driving test before they passed? What make and model cars, trucks, and motorcycles did you own? What memories were attached to them?

We had an old, blue Chevy station-wagon that had not only thousands of miles on the odometer but thousands of memories. Delivering newspapers during an icy winter when more than once it slid off the road into a ditch when the small town's snowplow budget was exhausted to family vacations. That car was such a trooper that even when we finally replaced it, a neighbor borrowed it, blown head-gasket and all. It was finally driven to the local dump spewing huge clouds of white exhaust, put up on blocks, and the wheels removed for the new tires purchased right before the engine blew. I literally cried when "Old Blue" was driven off for the final time. Most reliable car we ever had.

Was there one special place you went every Labor Day? Was Thanksgiving always at Grandma's or Auntie Belle's? What made it memorable? What about Disneyworld, Six Flags, Sea World and other theme parks? Was it a once in a lifetime trip or an annual pilgrimage?

Were all the kids crammed and fighting in the back of a Ford Taurus sedan? Or comfortably watching movies courtesy of that onboard DVD player in your Yukon Denali? Was your flying experience "cattle class" or first class?

It's not always something you want to remember, but it's another thing with historical value when you consider how long it took to travel twenty miles a hundred years ago in a Model-T across rutted country roads.

Modern flight schedules are filled with dichotomies as well. I've been on trips where it took as long to get from Houston, Texas to Oakland, California as it did from Houston to Amsterdam, The Netherlands. Not necessarily fun, but certainly part of the story.

I don't doubt that keeping kids entertained on long road trips has been a challenge since covered wagons. Wouldn't you just love to hear about *that* if your family was amongst the early pioneers? Were your vacations extravagant excursions abroad? Or within a few miles and held to a strict budget? Spontaneous or planned for years?

People, Activities, and Games

Who participated? Was it just the immediate family, extended family, entire neighborhood, grade school class, Sunday School class or who? Was there a certain person who usually took charge, was the star, or drove everyone crazy? Did you have family reunions? Was this where all the cousins got to know each other?

Were certain games a tradition, whether indoors or out? Poker, dominoes, Yahtzee, Canasta, Rummy? How about family softball or football debacles where someone almost always wound up in the emergency room? Did the TV go out in the middle of the Superbowl? What about Frisbee tournaments? Rockhounding? Camping? Spelunking? What does your family do for fun?

Did you ever pack for the beach and get hit with a late season snowstorm? It's been said regarding vacations to take half as many clothes and twice as much money, something you may want to editorialize about. Did you substitute a pumpkin for the football one year because Cousin Rob forgot it was his responsibility to bring the pigskin?

Special Clothing, Costumes or Equipment

Was Halloween a family affair? Was there a costume theme, such as *Star Wars* characters or simply M&Ms?

What about other holidays such as dressing up like pilgrims for Thanksgiving? Did you purchase your ski equipment and clothing at the end of the previous season when it went on sale or better yet, in a thrift shop?

Weather and Other Factors

Blizzards, floods, hurricanes, tornados, droughts, wildfires, and thunderstorms all add to the memories. Not all family history or folklore needs to be amusing. I was born during a blizzard that held the record that lasted until decades later.

Did you have any family rituals associated with preparations for tornado or hurricane season, such as drills or rotating the emergency food supply?

We kept our hurricane kit in the hall closet in a big plastic garbage can (a new one, of course) and rotate the canned food once a year. If we were ever in a position where we were depending on it, we didn't want it to be hopelessly out of date. It also got the kids involved so they understood the concept of preparedness and added some suggestions for the food involved.

I knew a family who spent a hurricane gridlocked on a Houston freeway because they waited until the last moment to evacuate. I never forgot that vicarious experience and made sure when subsequent severe storms arrived, I was one of the first ones out. A month after Hurricane Katrina hit New Orleans, Hurricane Rita was bearing down on Houston with all the delicacy of a freight train.

Did we stick around?

Ya think?

Nope, we were enjoying lakefront living in the Hill Country, watching miles upon miles of backed-up traffic on satellite TV while those slower to decide sat stuck on the freeways.

What storms or natural disasters have you experienced? What did you learn from them? What experiences will stay with you forever? What bonding took place with others sharing the same event? Did it bring out the best or the worst of mankind? If you lost everything, what was the recovery like? Who are the ones who helped out when you needed it most and you'll never forget?

CHAPTER FIVE

Additional Categories

A S NOTED EARLIER, FEEL free to invent new categories as needed. Your personal collection does not need to fit some pre-established list with the caveat of planning to submit it to a repository. You can find more information pertaining to that from the resources in Appendix B.

Children's Stories/Jump Rope Rhymes

I don't know if kids even play jump rope anymore. If they do, then get them to tell you the rhymes. Better yet, make a short video of them performing. It will make them feel important to contribute and they'll be amusing to watch later and pass on to the next generation.

Nursery rhymes or fairy tales could be included, especially any favorites. Pictures or videos are a must. Wouldn't you love to see a picture of your mother's face as a toddler while her grandmother read her favorite story?

Years ago, it wasn't as easy as it is today to record such events. Even if you haven't done it yourself, I'm sure you know someone who's done just that and posted it to Facebook. Some people post so much to Facebook that it would make a family history far too cumbersome. If that's the case, choose the one you consider the highlight of the week or month for long-term preservation.

Verbal Traditions

Grandpa's Italian accent and misunderstandings created by it or how well Uncle Guido could imitate Grandpa when he lost his temper all belong here. Learning a new language is usually rich with stories, but even if the only language your family has ever spoken is the same one they employ today, there will be something unique to consider.

Is your family bilingual? Can you understand a language yet not speak it? I once worked with a woman who was born in Mexico yet came to the USA at a young age. One time I asked her to translate something into Spanish and she admitted she didn't speak it because her father insisted they learn to speak English and would actually beat them if they didn't. Not only did she learn English, but she was actually unable to speak Spanish later in life when it would have benefited her career to do so, probably due to those early experiences.

What expressions are common in your family? Was language always proper or more colorful? Was Grandpa awake all night "like a tree full of owls?" Was your mother on you "like white on rice" if you forgot to say "please?" What part of the country is your family from? Did your father speak with a Texas drawl or sound more like a Brooklyn cop? Descriptions like this make a person come alive.

Games and Entertainment

Which games did your family enjoy? These could include commercial games such as Scrabble, Yahtzee, Uno, Bridge, Poker, Monopoly, Dominoes or any other family favorites. Were there any related funny stories, even if it's only associated with one session in particular? Did you family get together every Friday for a game of nickel-dime poker?

If you're raising a family today, entertainment is probably very different and may include video games or simply watching cable or satellite television. If that's the case, you might want to make a list of your favorite programs. The better ones will live forever via syndication, and it might be interesting to your descendants to see yours or your family's favorite programs show up on the air decades later.

Another list worth keeping is favorite movies, including which ones are popular icons for the age, such as the *Star Wars, Indiana Jones, Harry Potter, Twilight,* or *Hunger Games* series. Anything that is part of the popular culture for the day is worth preserving.

Some of my favorite pictures of my mother are those that show her in the typical dress of the "Roaring Twenties."

Gardening

What are your memories associated with flowers, herbs, berries, vegetables or fruit trees? Is there anything your family simply *has* to plant every year? Why? Flavor, seasoning, nutrition or good luck? What memories do you have of Grandma's garden? Was it perfect, row by row, or more casual, meandering through the flowers and shrubs?

One of my favorite gardening stories involved when my kids were supposed to be shelling peas, got bored, and fed them to the calf. Or the fact when they were sent out to pick peas they ate more than they brought inside, which was my own sneaky way of getting them to eat them at all. Another favorite was finding a tiny fawn asleep in the cabbage patch.

What about foraging? Did you pick wild asparagus every spring? As a kid in the New York Hudson Valley, my friends and I feasted on wild berries in the woods.

Was gardening easier then or now? Is the weather different or do you live in a different place?

Beliefs/Superstitions

These can be serious or as silly as you can get, whether it's throwing spilled salt over your shoulder or "step on a crack, break your mother's back." Wearing a certain color on a specific day of the week could have inherent meaning as well. Remember the significance of those green M&Ms?

Are you or any relative psychic, into tarot, astrology, ghosts, UFOs or a candidate for the next Nostradamas? Is it accepted as normal, respected or somewhat of a family joke? Did you ever live in a house you were sure was haunted? What experiences led you to that conclusion?

What about religion? Is there a long-standing tradition, one that's been lost, or a new one developing? Any interesting conversion stories? Pilgrimages to sacred locations?

Pets

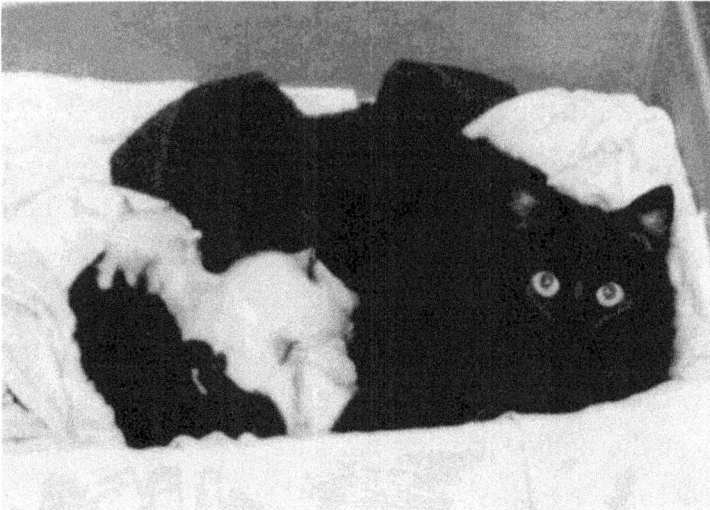

Most families have had at least one beloved pet. These are not limited to the more-typical cat or dog, but can include fish, hedgehogs, guinea pigs, ant farms, snakes, spiders (yuck), and so forth.

Where did your pet get its name? Why was it unique? What stories do you have that illustrate its personality? How did it come into your life? How did you mourn its demise? These are often the most endearing and memorable of family stories that span the emotional spectrum from hilarious to heartbreaking.

Even fish have personalities, something that surprised me. We had a betta that would eat out of your hand. One time I had some cichlids, which are aggressive and often establish a pecking order where one becomes the scapegoat, who usually doesn't survive.

I had this situation but refused to accept nature's cruelty. I would put the poor victim in an excluder while his gnawed-off fins and tail grew back. Like most nerds, Homer was far more intelligent than his tormenters. I'm glad I actually had a witness to his antics. He would jump out, tease his peers in a fishy, *You can't catch me!* sort of way, then jump back into the excluder, where he'd stare out at the bullies in what I'm sure was a fish version of *neener-neener.*

Were any family members in a 4-H Club? Did anyone ever raise an animal, get so attached to it they couldn't part with it at auction, and it became an unlikely family pet? Did you ever make the mistake of naming a farm animal destined to slaughter? What animal stories does your family have?

Cheers and Chants

Family cheers can be as unifying and fun as they are at a high school or college football game. If you don't have one consider making one up, especially if you have kids. We had one that went "We'll do good and never harm, Father Fox's Funny Farm" followed by calling off the names of all the kids, eldest to youngest.

If football or some other sport was important to your family, you may also want to include those from the specific schools, if nowhere else in the personal histories of those who attended that particular institution.

Rituals/Initiations

For weddings there's the "Something old, something new, something borrowed and something blue" tradition, but perhaps you have one that's more original. Sweet Sixteen parties, Proms, or other rites of passage all fit into this category. Homecoming dances in most of Texas involve elaborate corsages decked with long ribbons, flowers, trinkets and all sorts of things. What about Gender Reveal activities to announce the sex of that bun still in the oven?

Pranks

This one is particularly fun, especially years later when they've been hopefully forgiven, if not long forgotten. Did anyone in your family ever dress up like Darth Vader and scare the living daylights out of their neighbor who'd just come home from a long night on graveyard shift? Toilet paper a neighbor's lawn to celebrate her thirtieth birthday? Leave a dead skunk in a mailbox or tied beneath a car? Trap a raccoon in a suitcase left on a pool table then abandoned as if forgotten, then waiting in the parking lot for the fun to begin? Limburger cheese on the manifold of the groom's honeymoon car?

Expressions

These cover a broad spectrum, whether it's a unique way to say, "Excuse me" or expressions like those mentioned above under "Verbal Traditions" such as "he was on me like white on rice" or "I was up all night like a tree full of owls." Theses can be related to the times or the area. One I recall from my college years related to the icy gales that pummeled Utah State University in the winter, which stated, "Canyon winds don't blow, Logan sucks."

Expressions can capture a time or a culture in a concise and memorable way. A family expression we had was "place-backs." I had six children which resulted in seating problems in the family room. If someone had to leave and they didn't want to relinquish their seat the "rule" was if they said "place backs" when they got up, then no one else could take the seat. Another family with a similar problem would touch the back of their chair and simply say "saved."

Practices

This is another broad category that can include a variety of traditions such as wedding or baby showers, recycling, the "rag bag," starting a savings account for the grandkids, or birthday presents (such as a dollar for each year of age) to name a few. Hobbies, especially those enjoyed by several members of a family such as model building, antique auto restoration, hunting, fishing, camping, and so forth can all be included here. Trades and skills passed along whether it's carpentry or welding are worth capturing as well. Does your family own a business? What makes it unique?

Jokes

Humor can be found everywhere, whether it's on the job or at church. This includes anything that makes you laugh, whether it's a cartoon or story. One example that comes to mind is a picture I had of a two-story outhouse with the top level labeled "Management" and the bottom labeled "Workers." My management was not amused and I was told to take it down. I wonder to this day where their sense of humor was.

An example of a religious based joke was a scripture in Zechariah 5:1 – 3 that became known as the "TP Scripture" (TP is short for "toilet papering.") In the King James version it reads, "Then I turned, and lifted up mine eyes, and looked, and behold a flying roll." In some families it was the "Food Fight" scripture. Another one was the "Fly Scripture" from Isaiah 6:5 that states "Then said I, Woe is me for I am undone."

Examples of occupational or perhaps college humor can be seen on the show "The Big Bang Theory." As a physics major myself, I remember numerous witty sayings we'd see displayed in our study area such as "Physicists have no GUTS" (referring to Grand Unified Theories) or "Physicists have strange quarks" (referring to the sub-atomic particles). "May the Net Force be With You," "Heisenberg might have slept here," "Blackholes Suck," "Earn big profits as a fully trained quantum mechanic," and so forth are other examples.

Gestures

I hesitate to go into this one for fear of wandering off into offensive territory, but any teenager and most likely family certainly has a few stories that relate to body emissions at inappropriate times or funny faces behind Mom's back when she served a certain unpopular dish such as liver.

From my high school days in California in the 1960s we had several other than the well-known "middle finger salute" that remains popular to this day. One was to put one hand behind your head, fingers visible over the top, the other extended in front of you in the direction of the recipient, fingers on both hands wiggling. Even if I remembered what it meant, it would probably be politically incorrect and I'd probably refuse to divulge it, especially in writing. Hitting the bottom of your chin with the back of your hand was another one that undoubtedly had uncomplimentary connotations.

A warning gesture in our family relative to body emissions involved tucking in the middle three fingers with the thumb and pinkie extended, then placing the thumb in the middle of your forehead or the end of your nose. Everyone else was to acknowledge the warning with the same gesture and it was "bad" to be last. This gesture became so ingrained in our family that I once saw one of my children do it in her sleep when she was around three years old.

Nicknames and Labels

This one could likewise get out of hand but might be worth it a few years down the road. These are especially relevant to family history when the name stuck, such as "Butthead." I'm sure you know at least one nickname in this category. Teenagers in particular seem to have a rich storehouse of names. A few I remember are frump, gorp and snarf. I'll spare you the definitions.

Legends

These may not be directly related to family members but cover experiences with the local culture. They can be humorous or dead serious, fact or fiction. A haunted house or forest, UFO sightings, or an event that the area will always remember, all fit here.

One of the most interesting facets of local legends is how similar they tend to be, regardless of where you live. In the adolescent category, nearly every region has at least one that involves someone getting killed, usually in a car wreck. These victims become "folk heroes" with the repeated telling of the story often introducing various distortions and exaggerations.

Nonetheless, they tend to represent certain archetypes that become more interesting as their theme repeats, generation to generation. Thus, what may not seem that interesting now, may be in twenty years, due to either still being around or the sudden appearance of a new updated version.

Music

What musical talents (or lack thereof) does your family represent? In this day of computers, televisions, and iPads music doesn't represent the entertainment medium it once did for families when they would gather around the piano or guitar each evening and sing together.

Nonetheless, if your family does have a musical tradition, include it in your family history, whether it's dancing, composing, singing, or playing a musical instrument. A video is a must, especially for that first band concert, recital, or when Mary Beth sang "The Star-Spangled Banner" at the start of a football game, whether it was a high school, college, or especially for an NFL team.

I cherish the picture I have of my concert pianist maternal grandmother at the keyboard. It's placed on my own piano, even though she would roll over in her grave to hear my pitiful attempts. School band, orchestra and drill/dance team efforts along with their excursions are rich with stories, particularly field trips and competitions.

Children's Songs

Here's another area where kids can get involved. Often their songs make adults cringe when they get kind of, well, gross and disgusting. On the other hand, maybe you taught them to your children as part of your family's tradition! Here are a few verses from my kids' generation sung to the tune of *"Allouette"* as an example (which, incidentally, was taught to them by an adult neighbor):

(Chorus)

Suffocation, super suffocation
Suffocation, the game we like to play.
On your head a plastic bag
Pretty soon you start to gag
You turn blue, then you're through
Oh, oh, oh, oh....
(Chorus)
Find yourself a rubber hose
Then you put it up your nose
Turn it on, then you're gone,
Oh, oh, oh, oh....
(Chorus)
You are playing hide and seek
Gee, that fridge looks really neat
Fall asleep, six feet deep,
Oh, oh, oh, oh....

Filksongs

I'm sure many of you are scratching your head on this one. These are similar to children's songs but typically sung by older participants. Usually, they take the melody of a familiar song with different words. If they tell a story, they're a filksong. Otherwise, they're known as parodies. Weird Al Yankovic actually made a living with this practice with numerous others following suit on YouTube.

Coming up with the lyrics will usually require someone with poetic license, but kids can usually produce something. If your family has any good ones no doubt the younger generation has already shared it on YouTube. Be sure to capture it for your family history as well.

Family History Research

Undoubtedly, if you're into family history you've had a variety of interesting experiences finding information, distant cousins, unusual leads, visits from beyond the grave, or a relative who refuses to cooperate because they don't want to reveal those "skeletons in the closet." Don't forget to include these as well, they'll be among the most popular and oft-repeated sections. What could be more charming than to have a distant relative who was a hero or even a pirate, as the case may be?

One of my favorites was when I discovered that one of my great-great-great-grandfathers was a steamboat captain on the Hudson River. Another story claimed one of my ancestors survived being swallowed by a whale.

Inspirational

It goes without saying that inspirational experiences belong in a family history. There is nothing more meaningful to future generations than hearing of the struggles of the ones who went before. That orange crate furniture you had to get through college, the clunker you drove, shopping in K-Mart on Christmas Eve when everything was on sale, all become cherished stories.

At some point nearly every family will encounter hard times and knowing others survived and better yet, how, can be of great comfort. Is there a certain story or person who changed your life? What did you learn and how did it affect you?

Vacations

This is similar to the "Trip" category. It's up to you to decide whether there's a distinct difference. Regular excursions, such as those for the holidays, are more of a "trip" while "vacations" are more unique, perhaps even once in a lifetime events.

The more these resemble a Chevy Chase movie from the 80s the better, according to the formula *Crisis + Time = Humor*. One of ours that comes to mind was a trip destined for the Grand Canyon that didn't turn out as planned. Our transmission went out, which resulted in an unexpected layover in Flagstaff, Arizona while the car was repaired. These people were so familiar with the problem that there was a transmission shop on every corner.

The motel we were staying in overlooked a freeway and some poor soul decided to end it all by walking out in front of an eighteen-wheeler while we were there, which my daughter witnessed and is traumatized by the gruesome scene to this day, decades later. By the time we got to the Grand Canyon, time was running out and our three-day stay was reduced to three hours. The good news was that we arrived just before sunset, found the perfect lookout point, and enjoyed that inspiring scene accompanied by someone playing the bagpipes. We got quality, if not quantity, and numerous memories.

Arts and Crafts

What artistic abilities are there in your family? If there something in particular that has become a multi-generational pastime, such as making quilts or birdhouses? This is where pictures are truly worth a thousand words since it would be highly impractical to maintain a sample of everything in this category.

My mother was an artist and while I have several of her pastels and paintings, I can't find room for the ones I have. My children all have a few, and fortunately, I have photos of the many she sold over the years. Any competitions, showings, newspaper clippings and such can serve as encouragement for subsequent generations pursuing similar endeavors.

Sports

This can be anything from watching a game on TV and Superbowl parties to tennis, golf, croquet, swimming, martial arts, boating, fishing, hunting, ice or rollerskating, etc. Anything your family enjoys together. Note any traditions, special events, experiences and so forth whether they involved a college, commercial, high school or local team.

Of course, the more personalized the experience the better, like the time your son made the winning touchdown at the big regional championship game. The more you involve your children in compiling family folklore the more interested they'll be and it will certainly have more meaning years hence when they're working on preserving memories of their own family.

Ethnic Heritage

If your family has ethnic ties, these are important to chronicle, especially since they may get lost over the generations. There are several sources listed in Appendix

B that could provide more ideas. Mostly they'll fit into the other categories but if not, be sure to include them here.

Fashion

Don't you love those old pictures with outrageous hair styles and clothing that make you wonder what you could have possibly been thinking at the time? Even if you can't remember the date, you can guess pretty close based on appearance. These are usually naturally captured through photographs of other occasions, so any related stories with some entertainment value are worth recording.

CHAPTER SIX

Format

SINCE THIS IS PRIMARILY for your family's record and enjoyment, the format is largely open to whatever you want it to be. Preserving memories in scrapbooks is great, but bear in mind that if you have more than one child it may cause a fight later.

One thing we did to try and prevent that was to give each of our children a photo album. Whenever we'd take pictures (back in the old days of prints) we'd divide them up so that everyone had at least a few to represent those big occasions, such as holidays and vacations.

Now, with digital media, it's easiest to compile them onto a CD, flashdrive, or some other form of electronic media and make sure everyone has a copy. But remember what I said in the section on obsolescence! Whatever you do otherwise is correct, the only way to do it incorrectly is not to do it at all.

CHAPTER SEVEN

Finding Inspiration

FOR A LISTING AND description of various repositories and groups related to folklore/folklife refer to Appendix B. If you live near one, it might be an interesting fieldtrip that brings inspiration for your own project or perhaps the boost you need to get started.

You may also be interested to know that some of the repositories welcome submissions. If, perchance, you want to share your family's folklore in this manner, then you'll need to check with them for preferred format. One that I'm familiar with contains the name of the contributor, genre, a title, some background/ biographical information on the person providing the information, and any necessary contextual data so it makes sense.

If that is in the farthest reaches of your mind at this point, you might want to find out, anyway. That way your work conforms to the standard, just in case. It would probably be a major job to adapt your work after-the-fact. Then if you decide to share it later, you'd be good to go.

Appendix A

FAMILY FOLKLORE IDEA COLLECTION SHEET

*Y*OU CAN GET AN electronic copy of this table for free by sending an email with "FHFF Idea Collection Sheet" in the subject line to *marcha@kallioperisingpress.com*. I'll send you one in pdf format that will make it even easier for you to send a copy to family members to gather their memories, too.

FAMILY FOLKLORE IDEA COLLECTION SHEET

HOLIDAY or OCCASION	Foodways	Trip, Location & Transportation	People, Activities or Games Involved	Special Clothing, Costumes or Equipment	Weather and Other Factors
New Years Eve and New Years Day					
Superbowl					
Presidents' Day					
Martin Luther King Day					
Valentine's Day					
St. Patrick's Day					
Easter					
Spring Break					
Spring Equinox					

HOLIDAY or OCCASION	Foodways	Trip, Location & Transportation	People, Activities or Games Involved	Special Clothing, Costumes or Equipment	Weather and Other Factors
May Day					
Memorial Day					
Graduation					
Weddings					
4th of July					
First Day of School					
Labor Day					
Halloween					
Veteran's Day					
Thanksgiving					
Christmas and Christmas Eve					
Hanukah					

HOLIDAY or OCCASION	Foodways	Trip, Location & Transportation	People, Activities or Games Involved	Special Clothing, Costumes or Equipment	Weather and Other Factors
Births and Birthdays					
Deaths and Funerals					
Awards and Recognition					
Military Deployments					
Sporting Events					
Dance, Band and Orchestra Recitals					
Moving					

Appendix B

THE FOLLOWING LINKS ARE to excellent online resources for ideas and guidance during your quest.

Smithsonian Education: Includes various guidelines such as interviewing ideas and ethics.

http://www.smithsonianeducation.org/migrations/seek2/family.html

Genealogy Forum: Includes a printable interviewing guide and questionnaire.

http://www.genealogyforum.rootsweb.com/gfaol/resource/Folklore.htm

Michigan State University: Excellent article on how to collect memories including interview techniques.

https://www.canr.msu.edu/news/how-do-you-capture-a-lifetime-of-memories

Michigan State University Extension: Downloadable Guidebook to the 4-H "Folk Patterns" Project.

https://www.canr.msu.edu/uploads/files/4H1330FamilyFolklo reActivitySheets.pdf

Library of Congress: Information on the American Folklife Center

https://www.loc.gov/research-centers/american-folklife-center/about-this-research-center/

[NOTE:—These were updated since the original version of this book was published with all of them active links as of March 2025]

About the Author

Marcha Fox is the mother of six children, seventeen grandchildren, and at last count, eleven great-grandchildren and counting. She earned a Bachelors' Degree in physics from Utah State University, where she first discovered family folklore while also attaining a minor in English.

A prolific writer, she's the author of the *Star Trails Tetralogy* science fiction series (https://StarTrailsSaga.com); the *Dead Horse Canyon Saga* (https://Dead-Horse-Canyon.com) with Northern Cheyenne coauthor, Pete Risingsun; as well as numerous articles and ebooks on a variety of subjects, which include, of all things, astrology (https://ValkyrieAstrology.com). Check out her blog at https://marcha2014.wordpress.com.

She retired in 2009 from a two-decade career as a NASA contractor in Houston, Texas where she worked a variety of positions including technical writer, engineer, supervisor, and manager. Since then, she devotes her time to writing, her cats, gardening, and various hobbies. She has lived in New York, California, Utah, and Texas and has recently gone full circle and returned to New York where she lives in an 1898 farmhouse in the Finger Lakes Region as part of a very lively three-generation household.

www.ingramcontent.com/pod-product-compliance
Lightning Source LLC
Chambersburg PA
CBHW070816280326

41934CB00012B/3201